FINDING RAY'S KEY

WRITTEN BY
SAM GODDARD

ILLUSTRATED BY
OWEN WILLIAMS

Published by
Filament Publishing Ltd
16, Croydon Road, Beddington,
Croydon, Surrey CR0 4PA
+44(0)20 8688 2598
www.filamentpublishing.com

"Finding Ray's Key" by Sam Goddard

© Sam Goddard 2018
Illustrations copyright Owen Arts Ltd

ISBN 978-1-912635-00-9

The right of Sam Goddard to be identified as the author of this work has been asserted by her in accordance with the Designs and Copyright act 1977 section 77.

All rights reserved
No part of the work may be copied in any way without prior written permission of the publishers.

Printed by IngramSpark

Dedicated to

Arthur and his Nana

Find free resources including

an audio download of this book

and more from Ray at:

www.findyourki.com

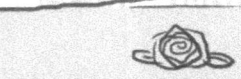

There was once a boy called Ray,

who didn't have much to say.

He didn't have much to do,

in fact he felt quite blue.

Often he would sit & wonder,

"What is this cloud I am under?"

But today, as he woke

He had a different thought,

For it was answers that he sought:

"What is the key to being happy?"

Ray had a sense that he needed

to find this "key"

that had sprung into his mind.

"A key, yes that's what I need," he said,

So a journey he started

as he got out of bed.

"Where do I start?

Hmm, who would know?"

He thought as he opened his door to go.

So he decided to walk to a forest nearby,

as usual looking down at his feet,

not up at the sky.

After walking a while he came to a place

where looking up at a tree

he thought he saw a face.

Surprised was Ray to see such a thing,

but even more so when then

he heard a bird sing.

He stopped a moment

as he was sure he heard whispers
on the wind...

"No, don't be absurd!"

"I am the key to make you happy."

Ray continued his walk on through the trees,

But today, he noticed the flowers and the bees.

Today, he noticed the sun up above,

Today, he noticed the earth underneath.

Ray stopped to wonder, "What was different today?"

And this time it was the trees he thought he heard say:

"I AM THE KEY _____ TO MAKE YOU HAPPY."

"How strange," he thought

as he continued to walk,

"Perhaps there's something wrong?"

"Not at all," he heard from a bird
up above,

"You are just hearing our song."

"I am the key to make you happy."

So he sat for a while and started to smile,

not something he did that much.

As he sat,

He then realized he felt quite bemused,

So he decided to lie down

For a bit of a snooze.

So he slept and fell into
                    a wonderful dream

where he met a young boy,
                    familiar he seemed.

The boy in his dream started to fade

and the daydream began to come to an end.

"Wait!" Ray cried, "what do you mean, I am the key?

For I can see that you, are me!"

The key he was seeking he had finally found,

It was within him and all around.

Ray stood and stretched and took a deep breath and decided to head back home.

He looked up to see no cloud above

Then closed his eyes and in his heart he felt only love.

"I AM STARTING TO SEE THAT THIS KEY
IS MINE

BUT IT IS ALSO ALL AROUND.

I AM THE KEY TO MAKE ME HAPPY,

AND THE KEY IS WHAT MAKES
THIS WORLD SHINE…"

About the Author:

Sam is a Reiki Master Teacher whose son Arthur inspired her to set up a Reiki school in Devon, a place where she shares her passion for Reiki with children and grown-ups.
www.devonschoolofreiki.co.uk

About the Illustrator:

Owen feels very lucky to live and work in the beautiful Devon countryside. He has illustrated a number of books for grown-ups and children. This is his first with Sam (and Ray).
www.akaowenarts.com

www.ingramcontent.com/pod-product-compliance
Lightning Source LLC
Chambersburg PA
CBHW042034100526
44587CB00029B/4422